WHICH?

C555061008

KINGFISHER

First published 2011 by Kingfisher
an imprint of Macmillan Children's Books
a division of Macmillan Publishers Limited
20 New Wharf Road, London N1 9RR
Basingstoke and Oxford
Associated companies throughout the world
www.panmacmillan.com

Illustrated by Ray Bryant
Concept by Jo Connor

ISBN 978-0-7534-3114-6

Copyright © Macmillan Children's Books 2011

All rights reserved. No part of this publication may
be reproduced, stored in or introduced into a retrieval
system, or transmitted, in any form or by any means
(electronic, mechanical, photocopying, recording or
otherwise), without prior written permission of the
publisher. Any person who does any unauthorized
act in relation to this publication may be liable to
criminal prosecution and civil claims for damages.

10 9 8 7 6 5 4 3 2 1
1TR/0511/LFG/UNTD/140MA

A CIP catalogue for this book is available
from the British Library.

Printed in China

This book is sold subject to the
condition that it shall not, by way
of trade or otherwise be lent, resold, hired
out, or otherwise circulated without the
publisher's prior consent in any form
of binding or cover other than that
in which it is published and without
a similar condition including this
condition being imposed on the
subsequent purchaser.

WHAT'S IN THIS BOOK?

WHICH . .

Did you know...

Many cave animals are blind. They do not need sight because they live in total darkness.

While we were searching for all those answers, we found out some other pretty interesting things, too. We wrote them all down on these panels – so you can memorize these facts and impress your friends!

We also thought it might be fun to see how much of this shiny new knowledge you can remember – so at the back of the book, on pages 56 and 57, you'll find some Quick-Quiz questions to test you out. It's not as scary as it sounds – we promise it'll be fun. (And besides, we've given you all the answers on pages 58 and 59.)

Are you ready for this big adventure? Then let's go!

WHICH IS THE HOTTEST PLANET?

Did you know...

Venus is covered by clouds of gas, which act like a big blanket, keeping in the Sun's heat.

Venus is the hottest planet, even though Mercury is closer to the Sun. The temperature on Venus can reach 500°C – that is eight times hotter than it gets in the Sahara (a desert), the hottest place on Earth.

WHICH IS THE COLDEST PLANET?

Did you know...

Pluto used to be known as the coldest planet. Then, in 2006, scientists decided that it was too small to count as a planet. Now Pluto is called a dwarf planet instead.

Neptune is the coldest planet. It is about 30 times further from the Sun than the Earth is. Temperatures on Neptune can get as low as -200°C. Neptune is also the planet with the fastest winds - they whip along at 2,160 kilometres per hour.

WHICH BIRD FLIES UNDERWATER?

Did you know...

Penguins cannot breathe underwater. Every few minutes they come back to the surface to take in a breath of air.

Penguins cannot fly through the air because their wings are too short and stumpy. They are much more at home in the ocean, where they use their wings as flippers. They zip through the water, chasing fish and squid.

WHICH FISH HAS HEADLIGHTS?

Did you know...

Away from the shore, the ocean plunges to about 4 kilometres in most places. The deep sea is inky black, fridge-cold – and home to some real oddballs!

The anglerfish lives in the dark depths of the ocean. It has a long fin dangling in front of its face. At the end of the fin is a blob that glows. Small fish are drawn to the light, only to disappear into the anglerfish's big, gaping mouth.

WHICH WAS THE BIGGEST DINOSAUR?

The biggest dinosaurs were the sauropods, a group of lumbering plant-eaters that had incredibly long necks. One of the biggest was a species of Diplodocus that measured 45 metres long and was taller than a four-storey building.

Did you know...

Epidendrosaurus was one of the smallest known dinosaurs. It was about the same size as a sparrow!

WHICH DINOSAUR HAD THOUSANDS OF TEETH?

Did you know...

Many hadrosaurs had a hollow head crest. The crest was probably for display, and may also have amplified the dinosaur's calls (made them louder).

Hadrosaurs had lots of tiny teeth in tightly packed rows. When these dinosaurs ground their top and bottom jaws together, their teeth worked like vegetable graters. Hadrosaurs are sometimes called duck-billed dinosaurs, because of their beak-like snouts.

WHICH FROGS CAN FLY?

Did you know...

Tree frogs live in rainforests. Other forest gliders include the paradise flying snake and colugos, or flying lemurs.

Tree frogs can climb trees, and some kinds can even glide from one tree to another! These unusual frogs have big feet with long, webbed toes. When they spread their toes out, the webs of skin between them act like parachutes and help the frogs to glide.

WHICH ANIMAL HAS A MAGIC HORN?

In some countries, rhinoceros horn is thought to be magical and is ground up for medicines. Even though it is against the law to hunt rhinos, some people still do. This is because they get a lot of money for a rhino's horn.

Did you know...

On some nature reserves, rangers cut off the rhinos' horns. It does not hurt the rhinos, and it stops poachers from killing them.

13

WHICH CRAB BORROWS ITS HOUSE?

Did you know...

Decorator crabs drape their shells with seaweed and sponges. It is their way of hiding from enemies.

Most crabs are protected by a hard casing all over, but the hermit crab is a bit of a softy. Its shell is very thin, so it needs something tougher to make a safe home. It finds an empty shell and backs into it. Hey presto! A new house!

WHICH SEEDS SAIL AWAY?

Coconut palms grow near the sea, so the ripe coconuts often fall into the water. Protected by their hard shell, they float out to sea. Eventually, after several weeks or months, they wash up on a new beach where they sprout and start to grow.

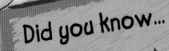

Did you know...

The double coconut palm, or coco de mer, grows on islands in the Indian Ocean. Its gigantic seeds weigh up to 20 kilograms each – as much as a sack of potatoes!

WHICH PLANT GROWS FASTEST?

Did you know...

A cycad tree in Mexico must hold the record as the slowest-growing plant. After 120 years, it was only 10 centimetres high!

Bamboo is the world's fastest-growing plant. Some kinds can grow nearly a metre per day. At that rate, they would reach the roof of a two-storey house in a week! The largest bamboos tower 40 metres high. It is hard to believe they belong to the same plant family as grass.

WHICH FORESTS HAVE THE TALLEST TREES?

The redwood forests that grow along the coast of California, USA, have the tallest trees. Redwood trees can grow to more than 100 metres tall – that is higher than a 30-storey building. The redwood forests receive plenty of rain that blows in from the Pacific Ocean.

Did you know...

Redwoods are some of the longest-lived trees on the planet. The oldest known example was cut down at the grand old age of 3,200!

WHICH PLANET IS KING?

Did you know...

Jupiter, Saturn, Uranus and Neptune are the furthest planets from the Sun. All four are made mostly of gas, and all four have rings around them.

The planet Jupiter is named after the ancient Roman king of the gods. Jupiter is by far the biggest planet in our solar system, measuring more than 140,000 kilometres across. It is so big that it is 2.5 times the size of all the other seven planets in the Solar System added together.

WHICH IS THE RED PLANET?

Did you know...

Mars is home to the largest-known volcano in the Solar System. Olympus Mons is 22 kilometres high and 700 kilometres across.

Mars, named after the Roman god of war, is often called the Red Planet. The ground there is covered in dusty red soil, which gets swept up by the wind to make pink clouds! The rocks on Mars have lots of iron in them, and iron goes red when it rusts. A better name for Mars might be the Rusty Planet.

WHICH IS THE SANDIEST DESERT?

Did you know...

The tallest sandcastle ever built stood more than 9 metres high – that is taller than five people standing on each other's shoulders!

The Sahara in North Africa is the largest hot desert in the world. Huge parts of it are covered with rolling hills of sand. Desert land is not always sandy, though. A lot of it is rocky or stony. Deserts are not always hot like the Sahara, either. To count as desert, they just have to be very dry. The biggest one, overall, is Antarctica – a dry, cold, desert continent.

WHICH RIVER WAS USED AS A ROAD?

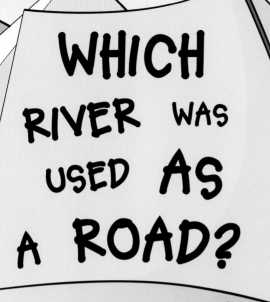

Did you know...

The only farmland in Egypt was by the Nile. This was known as the Black Land, because when the river flooded it left behind black mud.

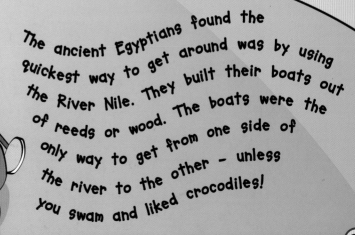

The ancient Egyptians found the quickest way to get around was by using the River Nile. They built their boats out of reeds or wood. The boats were the only way to get from one side of the river to the other – unless you swam and liked crocodiles!

WHICH IS THE BIGGEST OCEAN?

Did you know...

The Arctic is the smallest ocean – and also the coldest. For most of the year, it is covered in ice.

There are five oceans – the Pacific, the Atlantic, the Indian, the Arctic and the Southern. The Pacific ocean is by far the biggest. It is larger than the other four oceans put together, and also much deeper. It covers about a third of the whole of the Earth's surface.

WHICH VOLCANO BURIED A ROMAN TOWN?

Did you know...

Archaeologists made models of the people buried at Pompeii. They poured plaster into the spaces left in the rocks after bodies rotted away.

When Italy's Mount Vesuvius erupted in 79CE, ash fell like snow over the Roman town of Pompeii, burying it in 6-metre-deep drifts. Then it rained. The ash set like concrete, freezing the town in time. Pompeii was not seen again until digging began in the 1750s.

WHICH DINOSAURS HAD BODY ARMOUR?

Did you know...

Ankylosaurus was a plant-eater. Its armour gave it some protection from predators but it had another defence, too – a huge, bony tail club.

The thick, leathery skin on the top of Ankylosaurus's body had hard, bony lumps and spikes growing in it. This suit of body armour made the dinosaur into a living tank – very difficult to attack! Meat-eaters would have broken their teeth if they had tried to bite into Ankylosaurus's skin.

WHICH ANIMALS HAVE SKELETONS ON THE OUTSIDE?

Did you know...

Insects, centipedes, millipedes, spiders, scorpions, prawns, crabs and lobsters all have a tough exoskeleton.

Not all animals have a skeleton inside them to hold their body together. Animals that do not have a skeleton are called invertebrates. Many invertebrates have a tough skin called an exoskeleton. This 'outside skeleton' does the same job as an inside one. It protects and supports an animal's soft body.

WHICH PLANT FOOLS A FLY?

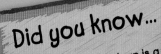

Did you know...

The Venus flytrap is a plant that springs a trap to catch its meal. Its hinged leaves snap shut if a fly brushes against one of their tiny, sensitive hairs.

Pitcher plants have jug-shaped leaves that tempt insects with a sugary smell. But the leaves are slippery traps. When a fly lands, it loses its footing, slips inside the 'jug' and drowns in a pool of juice. Pitcher plants grow on boggy ground where the soil is poor. They need their juicy snacks for extra nourishment.

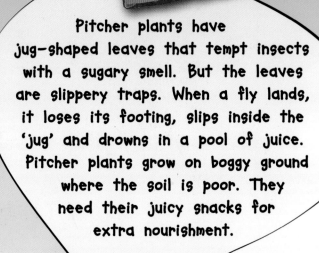

WHICH FLOWER FOOLS A BEE?

Did you know...

Many trees and grasses spread their pollen on the wind. They do not rely on animal visitors, so they do not need to grow colourful, sweet-smelling flowers in order to attract them.

A bee orchid's flowers look and smell just like female bees. Male bees zoom to the flowers, wanting to mate with them – but they have been tricked! The plant is using them as postal workers to deliver little packets of pollen to other orchids. When the pollen rubs off on another orchid, that flower can make seeds.

WHICH DRAGON LIVES UNDERWATER?

Did you know...

Like sea horses, sea dragon dads give birth. The female lays her eggs in the male's pouch and he guards them until they hatch.

The leafy sea dragon lives in warm seas off the coast of Australia. This relative of the sea horse is disguised to look like a piece of floating seaweed. Its body is covered by little flaps of skin that look like leafy fronds waving in the water.

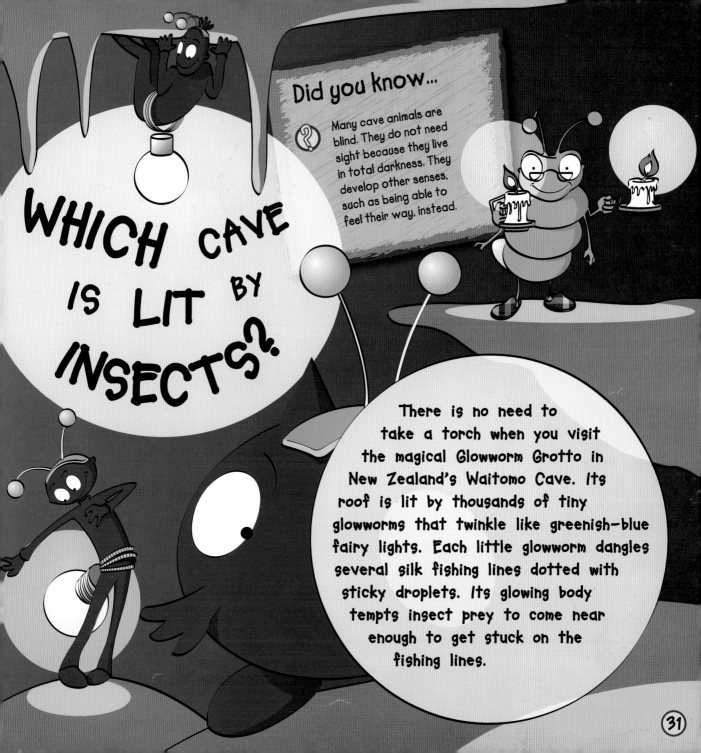

WHICH CAVE IS LIT BY INSECTS?

Did you know...

Many cave animals are blind. They do not need sight because they live in total darkness. They develop other senses, such as being able to feel their way, instead.

There is no need to take a torch when you visit the magical Glowworm Grotto in New Zealand's Waitomo Cave. Its roof is lit by thousands of tiny glowworms that twinkle like greenish-blue fairy lights. Each little glowworm dangles several silk fishing lines dotted with sticky droplets. Its glowing body tempts insect prey to come near enough to get stuck on the fishing lines.

31

WHICH ANIMAL CHANGES COLOUR?

Chameleons usually have browny-green skin, but it only takes them a few minutes to change their colour completely. These strange little lizards can match their surroundings, which helps them hide from enemies. They also change colour when they are frightened or angry. Chameleons watch out for danger with their amazing eyes, which swivel in different directions.

Did you know...

A chameleon catches its insect prey by shooting out its long, elastic tongue. The action is far too lightning-fast for the human eye to follow.

WHICH ANIMALS ARE REPTILES?

Did you know...

The world's biggest reptile is the saltwater crocodile. This huge beast can grow to as long as 7 metres, or longer.

Snakes, lizards, crocodiles and turtles all belong to the same animal group – the reptiles. All reptiles have a bony skeleton and a scaly skin. Most of them lay eggs, which hatch on land. But some reptiles give birth to their babies.

WHICH IS THE BIGGEST CREEPY-CRAWLY?

The Indonesian giant stick insect is the longest creepy-crawly in the world. At 33 centimetres long, it would only just fit inside the open pages of this book. The heavyweight champion of the insect world is the goliath beetle. It weighs about the same as a hamster.

Did you know...

Long ago, before the time of the dinosaurs, monster dragonflies cruised through the air. Some were the size of seagulls.

WHICH IS THE SMALLEST CREEPY-CRAWLY?

Did you know...

There are nearly a million known species of insects – but there may be as many as 10 million more that we have not discovered yet.

You would find it hard to see a fairy fly, because it is no bigger than a full stop. Most species are just 0.2 millimetres long. This insect is really a wasp, not a fly. The female lays her tiny eggs inside the eggs of other insects, such as cicadas, beetles and bugs.

WHICH IS THE WORLD'S MOST POPULAR SPORT?

Did you know...

National football teams have competed in the World Cup every four years since 1930, except for the years 1942 and 1946.

Footballs are kicked about in more than 200 countries around the world. The game is played by millions of people, in playgrounds, parks, streets and, of course, football grounds. The earliest football-like game dates back 2,400 years. It was called zuqiu, and it was played in ancient China.

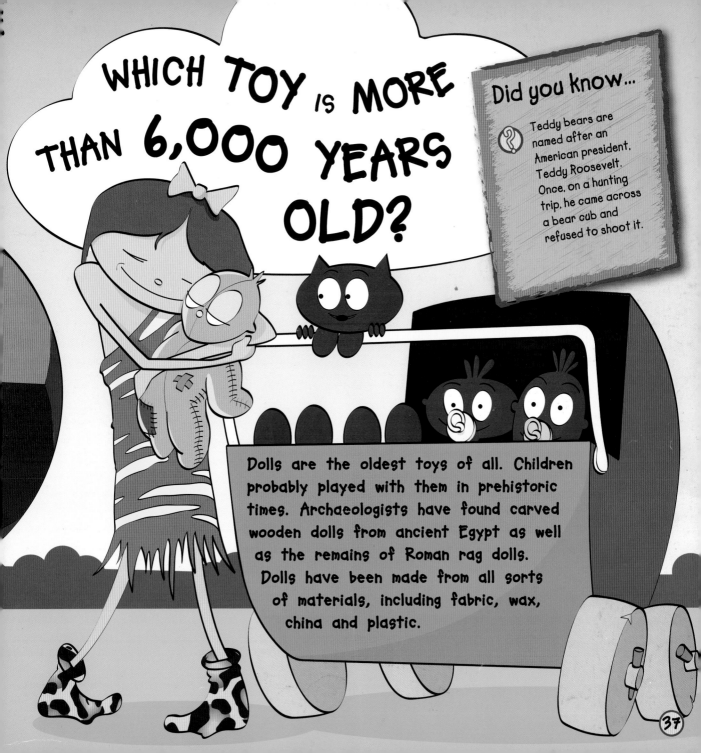

WHICH TOY IS MORE THAN 6,000 YEARS OLD?

Did you know...

Teddy bears are named after an American president, Teddy Roosevelt. Once, on a hunting trip, he came across a bear cub and refused to shoot it.

Dolls are the oldest toys of all. Children probably played with them in prehistoric times. Archaeologists have found carved wooden dolls from ancient Egypt as well as the remains of Roman rag dolls. Dolls have been made from all sorts of materials, including fabric, wax, china and plastic.

WHICH IS THE FASTEST CAR?

Did you know...

In 1899, a bullet-shaped electric car became the first-ever vehicle to travel faster than 100 kilometres per hour.

A British car called Thrust SSC set the world land speed record in 1997. Using two jet aircraft engines in place of a normal car engine, it reached 1,228 kilometres per hour. Thrust SSC was the first car to break the sound barrier (to travel faster than the speed of sound).

WHICH IS THE FASTEST BOAT?

Hydroplanes are speedboats that skim over the water, almost as if they are flying. In 1978, Ken Warby roared to 514 kilometres per hour in his jet-powered Spirit of Australia. This world record has never been broken!

Did you know...

In good winds, windsurfers can zip across the water at speeds of more than 80 kilometres per hour.

WHICH ARE THE BIGGEST TYRES?

Did you know...

In 1888, a Scottish vet called John Boyd Dunlop patented his design for air-filled bicycle tyres. Dunlop tyres are still being made today.

The world's biggest tyres are made for the huge dumper trucks that are driven on building sites. The air-filled tyres cushion the trucks' heavy loads of rock, gravel and earth. The tyres may be more than 3.6 metres high – that is about three times as tall as you are!

WHICH IS THE STEEPEST RAILWAY?

Did you know...

The world's highest railway links Tibet to the rest of China. One section, the Tanggula Pass, is more than 5,000 metres above sea level.

The view is fantastic on the Katoomba Scenic Railway in Australia's Blue Mountains, but the ride is pretty hairy! The railway is the world's steepest, dropping 415 metres in a little under two minutes. The railway line was built to carry miners down the steep slope, but today it transports tourists, instead – up to 84 at a time.

WHICH ARE THE TALLEST CRANES?

Did you know...

It is a long climb up to the cab of a tower crane. Some cabs have a toilet in them, to save the driver going up and down.

Tower cranes can reach higher than 15 houses piled on top of one another. When builders are putting up a skyscraper, they need a crane this tall to lift the beams, walls, windows and cladding into place.

WHICH CITY IS ON TOP OF A MOUNTAIN?

Did you know...

The Potala Palace towers above the streets of Lhasa. It is very grand. It has more than 1,000 rooms and even its roofs are made of gold!

The city of Lhasa is in Tibet, a region of China. Tibet borders the Himalayas, which are the world's highest mountains – so no wonder it is sometimes called the 'roof of the world'. Lhasa itself is 3,600 metres above sea level. It is built among the clouds, which blanket the city in a thick, wet mist.

WHICH ARE THE SMALLEST BOATS?

Did you know...

American Indians made round boats called bullboats by stretching buffalo skin over a frame of willow twigs. They used them to carry goods downriver.

Coracles are just about the world's smallest boats – they usually have room for only one person! Traditionally, these round boats were made from woven grasses, reeds or saplings and then, sometimes, made waterproof with a coat of tar.

WHICH CONTINENT CONTAINS THE MOST COUNTRIES?

Did you know...

The United Nations (UN) has 192 member countries. There are two independent nations – Kosovo and Vatican City – that are not UN members.

Africa contains more countries than any other continent – 53 of the world's 194 countries are found here. Many African countries are very new. In 1950, there were only 82 separate countries in the whole world.

WHICH HURRICANE BLEW THE HARDEST?

Did you know...

Hurricanes are given a name once their winds top 65 kilometres per hour. They are named in alphabetical order, with alternate girls' and boys' names.

The hurricane with the fastest recorded winds was Hurricane Wilma, in 2005. Its top wind speed was 295 kilometres per hour. Wilma killed 23 people. Hurricane Mitch, which struck in 1998, did not blow as hard but caused the deaths of more than 19,000 people.

WHICH IS THE WORLD'S BIGGEST CITY?

Did you know...

Every square kilometre in Tokyo is home to more than 2,600 people. No other city is so packed!

Tokyo, Japan, is the biggest city in the world. More than 36 million people live in Tokyo and its suburbs, with 13 million squashed into the city centre. Delhi in India and Sao Paulo in Brazil are the next two biggest cities. They are each home to more than 20 million people.

WHICH COMPUTER WAS AS BIG AS A BUS?

Did you know...

Today's pocket-sized mobile phones contain many, many times more computing power than early computers such as Colossus.

The first computer was about as long as four buses and was called Colossus. It was built in the United Kingdom and switched on in 1943. Very few people knew about it at the time because one of its first jobs was to crack secret codes.

WHICH BRIDGE CAN BREAK IN TWO?

London's Tower Bridge carries traffic over the River Thames. The road is built in two halves, which can be raised or lowered like drawbridges. When a tall ship sails up the river, each half of the bridge lifts up so that the ship can pass through.

Did you know...

Sydney Harbour Bridge, Australia, is the world's widest bridge. Two trains, eight cars, a cyclist and a person walking a dog can all cross it side by side.

WHICH IS THE BIGGEST INSTRUMENT?

Did you know...

The world's most valuable instruments are violins made more than 300 years ago by an Italian called Antonio Stradivari. Buying one costs more than a house!

The organ is the biggest musical instrument. The largest and loudest organ in the world is in Atlantic City, USA. It is so huge that it sounds as loud as 25 brass bands playing together. It has 12 keyboards and more than 33,000 pipes. Sadly, this record-breaking instrument does not work very well these days.

WHICH MOUSE IS MUSICAL?

Did you know...

The 18th-century composer Domenico Scarlatti claimed his pet cat helped to write his Cat's Fugue – when it tiptoed along the keys of his harpsichord.

The male grasshopper mouse of North America uses his shrill, chirrupping song to attract a mate. He stands up on his back legs and sings his heart out. It is his way of telling all the female mice around what a fine, strong mouse he is.

53

WHICH COUNTRY HAS MORE SHEEP THAN PEOPLE?

Did you know...

India is home to more than a quarter of all the world's cattle. More than 280 million cows and domestic buffalo live there.

Australia has more sheep than any other country. At the last count there were 110 million sheep – about five times the number of people. Neighbouring New Zealand has few people and around 40 million sheep. In fact, there are ten times more sheep than people in that country!

WHICH IS THE MOST CROWDED COUNTRY?

Monaco in southern Europe is famous for its motor racing, but it is also the most crowded country in the world. Its population of 35,400 people is packed into an area of less than two square kilometres. In comparison, Mongolia in central Asia is one of the emptiest countries. Only 1.7 people live in each square kilometre there.

Did you know...

The record for the world's smallest country is held by the Vatican City in Rome. It is only 0.44 square kilometres in size.

QUICK-QUIZ QUESTIONS

1. Mercury is the hottest planet. True or false?

2. Name a dwarf planet.

3. Unscramble RIPEN US ROUSE DAD to get the name of a tiny dinosaur.

4. How much does a coco de mer seed weigh?

5. Who was the ancient Roman king of the gods?

6. Which planet is home to the Solar System's biggest volcano?

7. Where is the Sahara?

8. The Pacific Ocean covers half of Earth's surface. True or false?

9. Unscramble US VIVE US to find the name of a volcano in Italy.

10. What do decibels measure?

11. What is an exoskeleton?

12. Where is Glowworm Grotto?

13. How do chameleons catch their dinner?

14. Which beetle weighs as much as a hamster?

15. When was the first-ever World Cup?

16. Which American president gave his name to toy bears?

17. How many jet engines did the fastest-ever car have?

18. Who drove the fastest-ever speedboat?

19. Unscramble SAINT SUN DOME AN to find a famous mountain range.

20. What is the name of the largest of the Hawaiian Islands?

21. Where is the Potala Palace?

22. What is a coracle?

23. How fast were Hurricane Wilma's winds?

24. Unscramble VARIANT STOOD IN AIR to find the name of a violin maker.

25. What is the world's smallest country?

QUICK-QUIZ ANSWERS

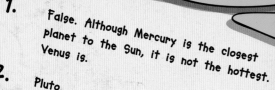

1. False. Although Mercury is the closest planet to the Sun, it is not the hottest. Venus is.

2. Pluto.

3. RIPEN US ROUSE DAD = Epidendrosaurus.

4. Up to 20 kilograms.

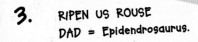

5. Jupiter.

6. Mars.

7. It is a desert in North Africa.

8. False. It covers a third of Earth's surface.

9. US VIVE US = Vesuvius.

10. Noise levels.

11. A tough outer skin that protects and supports an invertebrate's body.

12. Waitomo Cave, in New Zealand.

13. By shooting out their long, sticky tongue.

14. The goliath beetle.

15. In 1930.

16. Teddy Roosevelt.

17. Two.

18. Ken Warby.

19. SAINT SUN DOME AN = Andes Mountains.

20. Hawaii.

21. Lhasa, Tibet, in China.

22. A small, round boat.

23. They travelled at up to 295 kilometres per hour.

24. VARIANT STOOD IN AIR = Antonio Stradivari.

25. Vatican City.

TRICKY WORDS

ARCHAEOLOGIST
Someone whose job it is to find out about human history by finding and studying remains such as buildings and clothing.

CLADDING
The outer skin of a building, designed to keep out the weather and make the building look attractive.

COMPOSER
Someone who writes music.

CONTINENT
One of the Earth's seven main landmasses – North America, South America, Europe, Africa, Asia, Australia and Antarctica.

CORACLE
A small, round boat.

CYCAD
A primitive plant with a straight trunk topped by a crown of leathery leaves.

DECIBEL
A unit of measurement that indicates how loud a noise is.

DESERT
A dry region with little plant life.

DRAWBRIDGE
A bridge that is hinged at one end so that it can be raised and lowered.

EGYPTIANS
Ancient people who lived in Egypt, from around 5,000 to 2,000 years ago.

EXOSKELETON
The tough outer skin that protects the soft body of an invertebrate (spineless) animal.

FROND
The leaf-like part of seaweeds.

HADROSAUR
A two-legged dinosaur that had a duck-like beak and, usually, a head crest.

HARPSICHORD
A keyboard instrument popular in the 1700s and 1800s.

HURRICANE
A strong storm that forms over warm seas. Its winds travel at 120 kilometres per hour or more.

HYDROPLANE
A fast motor boat that travels just above the water.

INVERTEBRATE
An animal without a backbone (spine).

IRON
A hard, grey metal that reacts with moisture to form iron oxide, or rust.

JET ENGINE
An engine that burns fuel to produce a jet of hot gases that shoots out of the back of the engine, propelling the vehicle forwards.

LAVA
Liquid rock that spurts from volcanoes or cracks in the Earth's surface.

PATENT
To register an idea or invention with the government so that no one else is allowed to copy it.

PLANET
A large, ball-shaped object in space that orbits (travels around) a star. The Earth is a planet.

POACHER
Someone who hunts animals illegally.

POLLEN
Dust-like particles produced by a flower that contain its male sex cells. When pollen brushes against another flower, that flower can produce seeds.

PREDATOR
An animal that hunts and eats another animal.

PREHISTORIC
Describes the period of history before our written records began.

PREY
An animal that is hunted and eaten by another animal.

REDWOOD
An evergreen conifer tree, with reddish timber.

REPTILE
An animal with a backbone and a scaly skin. Most reptiles lay eggs on land, but some give birth to live young.

ROMANS
Ancient people from Italy who lived around 2,000 years ago in Europe, Africa and Asia.

SAUROPOD
A huge, long-necked, plant-eating dinosaur that walked on all fours.

SOLAR SYSTEM
The Sun and the objects in space that orbit it, including the eight planets.

SPEED OF SOUND
How fast sound travels through air - around 1,236 kilometres per hour.

SUBMERSIBLE
A small, underwater craft.

TAIL CLUB
A lumpy mass of bone at the end of an animal's tail, used in self-defence.

TAR
A black, sticky substance from rocks. Tar is used to coat road surfaces and to make boats waterproof.

VOLCANO
A vent (hole) in the surface or crust of a planet through which gas, ash and molten rock escape. The material that erupts can build up to form a mountain.

WORLD CUP
An international football competition that usually takes place every four years.

WHERE TO FIND STUFF

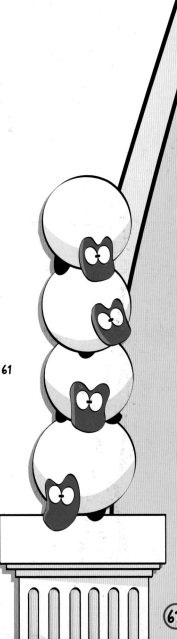